GW01090371

Around the

SOUTH AMERICA

Written by Antony Mason
Illustrated by Pauline Banazi

© 1994 Henderson Publishing Limited

Henderson
Woodbridge, England *Publishing*

LIST OF COUNTRIES

Argentina
Capital: Buenos Aires
Pop. 32,000,000
2,797,109 sq km
Currency: austral

Bolivia
Capital: La Paz
Pop.7,300,000
1,331,661 sq km
Currency: boliviano

Brazil
Capital: Brasília
Pop. 150,400,000
8,512,035 sq km
Currency: cruzado

Chile
Capital: Santiago
Pop. 13,200,000
738,494 sq km
Currency: peso

Colombia
Capital: Bogotá
Pop. 33,000,000
1,139,592 sq km
Currency: peso

Ecuador
Capital: Quito
Pop. 10,781,000
454,752 sq km
Currency: sucre

Guyana
Capital: Georgetown
Pop. 990,000
214,970 sq km
Currency: Guyanese dollar

Paraguay
Capital: Asunción
Pop. 4,300,000
406,630 sq km
Currency: guarani

Peru
Capital: Lima
Pop. 21,600,000
1,249,048 sq km
Currency: inti

Suriname
Capital: Paramaribo
Pop.436,000
163,256 sq km
Currency: guilder

Uruguay
Capital: Montevideo
Pop. 3,080,000
186,925 sq km
Currency: New Uruguayan
peso

Venezuela
Capital: Caracas
Pop. 19,700,000
912,050 sq km
Currency: bolivar

SOUTH AMERICA

Fourth largest
South America is the fourth largest of the seven
continents - almost twice the size of Europe, and
larger also than Antarctica and Australia.

World's biggest river
The mighty river Amazon crosses almost the entire
continent from west to east, 6448 km.
It has the largest volume of water of any river in
the world. An average of 120 million litres of water
pours from the Amazon into the Atlantic every
second - 60 times more than the Nile. This
represents one fifth of the world's river water.

The backbone of South America

The Andes mountains stretch almost the entire length of the west coast of South America - the longest mountain range in the world.
The highest mountain is Mount Aconcagua (6959 m), in the far west of Argentina.

Ice and steam

The Equator runs through northern South America. This means that much of the north has a hot, wet, tropical climate - but even here the Andes are often snow-capped. The south has a cooler, temperate climate, and the very south has bitterly cold winters.

Sharing out the world

At the start of the Great Age of European Exploration, the Spanish and the Portuguese decided to carve the world in two. A line was drawn down the Atlantic at about 2000 km from Europe. Any newly discovered territories to the east of the line would be Portuguese, and any to the west of it would be Spanish. As a result Brazil became Portuguese, but the rest of South America became Spanish - and that is how the languages of South America are divided today.

Amerigo - America

In 1501-2 an Italian navigator called Amerigo Vespucci explored the coast around the mouth of the River Amazon. Christopher Columbus thought that these new lands were part of the Far East.

Vespucci, however, concluded that they were a completely new continent, and mapmakers back in Europe named the continent after the Latin form of Vespucci's first name, Americus.

ARGENTINA

Favourable winds

The full name of Argentina's capital is Ciudad de la Santísima Trinidad y Puerto de Nuestra Señora la Virgen Maria de los Buenos Aires (City of the Most Holy Trinity and Port of our Lady the Virgin Mary of Favourable Winds). It is called Buenos Aires for short. Sailors needed favourable winds to bring their sailing ships to this port, founded in 1536. Today it is a modern, bustling place, one of the world's great cities, situated on the Rio de la Plata.

A hopeful name

Argentina's name comes from the Latin word for silver. The Italian-born British explorer Sebastian Cabot visited Río de la Plata (meaning 'silver river') in 1526 and sent some pieces of silver back to Spain. This created high hopes that the land was rich in silver. It wasn't - but instead Argentina later became rich through cattle and sheep farming, and grain.

Pampas

The huge grassy plains of central and northern Argentina are known as the Pampas (from an Indian word meaning 'plain').
It provides excellent pasture for huge herds of beef cattle, which are looked after by mounted cowboys called gauchos.

Maté time!

The traditional hot drink of the gauchos is maté, a bitter kind of tea made from the dried leaves of the maté tree.
Maté is served in a small pot with a straw-like pipe, and this is passed from person to person.

Wales in Patagonia

Patagonia is a vast, cold plateau in southern Argentina. There are Welsh sheep-farming communities in Patagonia, which were set up after 1865 to preserve Welsh culture and the Welsh language.

Land of Fire

The Portuguese navigator Ferdinand Magellan
(c.1480-1521) was the first to find a route from
the Atlantic Ocean into the Pacific in 1521. It was
a channel through the islands in the very south
of South America, between Tierra del Fuego and
the mainland. This channel is now called the Strait
of Magellan.

Tierra del Fuego means 'land of fire'. It was given
its name by Magellan because of the hundreds of
fires, lit by Indians, which he saw burning at night
along the coast.

Calm and fury

Magellan also gave the Pacific Ocean its name. It
means 'peaceful': in fact, it was so calm that his
crew nearly starved to death. On the other hand,
Cape Horn - at the southern tip of South America -
overlooks one of the most feared stretches of
ocean, where ships can encounter furious storms,
mountainous seas, and large chunks of icebergs.

Garden of the Andes

The region of north-west Argentina, around the city
of Mendoza, is the main wine-growing region. As
well as grapes, all kinds of fruit and vegetables are
grown here, including olives.

Mighty falls

One of the world's great waterfalls, the Iguaçu Falls, lies on the border between Argentina and Brazil, on the River Iguaçu. It is a cluster of 275 falls, dropping about 80 m down a horseshoe-shaped precipice.

Maradona!

Argentina has one of the world's leading football teams. It won the World Cup in 1978 and 1986, and was in the final in 1990. One of its most famous footballers is Diego Maradona (born 1960), who was the world's most valuable player during the 1980s.

That seals it!

The coast of southern Argentina is visited by elephant seals, the largest member of the seal family. Male elephant seals can be up to 6 m long and weigh 3600 kg.

'Don't cry for me, Argentina'
Eva Perón (1919-52) was the first wife of Juan
Domingo Perón (1895-1974), who was president
of Argentina from 1946 to 1955, and again from
1973 to 1974. Eva - known as Evita - was famous
for her beauty and immensely popular for her
charitable work for the poor, but she died of
cancer aged 33.

Islas Malvinas
These islands, known to British people as
the Falkland Islands, lie 770 km east of Argentina.
Around 2000 Falklanders make their livings from
sheep farming and fishing.
The Falkanders want the islands to remain a British
Crown Colony. In 1982 the Argentinian army
invaded the islands, but were pushed out by the
British army three months later after a brief war
which cost 1000 lives.

Freedom fighter
Argentina was the birthplace of José de San Martín
(1778-1850), one of the great leaders in the fight
against Spanish rule. He helped to win
independence for Chile and Peru.

CHILE

Long and thin
Chile occupies half of the west coast of South
America. It is 4100 km long from tip to toe, and
never more than 400 km wide - in places only
25 km wide!
The climate ranges from the hot Atacama desert in
the north to the icy wastelands of the south.

Cable car to the top
The capital of Chile, Santiago, was founded
in 1541, and its cathedral was built in 1558.
Overlooking the city is San Cristóbal Hill (228 m),
on which stands a huge statue of the Virgin Mary.
The summit can be reached by a cable car from
the city.

Earthquakes and volcanoes
The Andes mark a fault line in the earth's crust,
which often suffers from earthquakes. In 1906
Chile's chief port, Valparaíso, was destroyed by an
earthquake. There are also a number of volcanoes.

Very dry
The Atacama Desert in N. Chile is one of the world's driest places. It usually has no rain at all. No rain was recorded there during the 400 years up to 1971.

Indian country
Chile had a large Indian population before the arrival of the Spanish conquistadors in the 1530s and 1540s. Many died through wars and maltreatment, but mainly through diseases introduced by the Europeans. Chile's reduced Indian population live in Los Lagos province, named after its beautiful lakes, set against a backdrop of mountains. Their language is Araucanian.

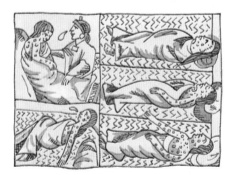

It's a fair copper
Chile is the world's largest producer of copper. Chuquicamata has the largest open-cast copper mine in the world.

Monkey puzzle

Monkey puzzle trees come from Chile. Their Latin name is Araucaria Araucana. Their stiff, sharp leaves are supposed to present a great problem to any monkeys wanting to climb them.

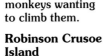

Robinson Crusoe Island

In 1704 the English buccaneer William Dampier abandoned an unpopular crew member, Alexander Selkirk, on some remote islands called Juan Fernandez. Selkirk spent four years on one of these islands before he was rescued. His account of his experiences intrigued the English author Daniel Defoe, who used it as the basis for his famous book Robinson Crusoe, published in 1719.

The chinchillas of Chile

A chinchilla is a rabbit-like rodent that lives in the Andes of Chile, Bolivia and Peru. Its bluish-grey fur is extremely soft and very valuable - which is why chinchillas were driven close to extinction. Now they are protected by law from hunting.

URUGUAY

Switzerland of South America
There was once great hope for Uruguay: it
was small, rich, and neutral - just like Switzerland.
However, in recent decades Uruguay has suffered
from a faltering economy, strikes, high inflation,
terrorist attacks and a repressive military
government.

One-city country
The only city of any size in Uruguay is the capital,
Montevideo. Founded by the Spanish in 1726, it
now has a population of about 1.5 million - nearly
half the total population of the whole country.

Wool and meat
Most of Uruguay is pasture, where huge herds of
sheep and cattle are grazed.
The main exports are meat, wool and leather. As in
Argentina, the ranches are called estancias, and the
cattle are herded by gauchos.

Corned Beef

Corned beef is one of the best known products of the cattle farms of South America - and was a particularly important export before the days of freezing and refrigeration. The beef is cooked then preserved in salt water (corned), before it is put into cans.

... and for pudding?

Uruguay grows a large amount of rice. It also has extensive orchards where oranges, tangerines, pears and peaches are grown.

Battle of the River Plate

In 1939, during World War II, a famous naval battle ended in the River Plate, near Montevideo. The British fleet cornered the German battleship Graf Spee, which had been attacking merchant ships in the Atlantic. The Graf Spee was damaged, but the Uruguayans refused to help. So the ship was deliberately sunk by its captain, who then shot himself.

PARAGUAY

Middle America
Paraguay is a landlocked country, surrounded by Brazil, Bolivia and Argentina. However, ocean-going ships can reach the capital, Asunción, by sailing up the river Paraguay.

A costly war
Paraguay became fully independent of Spain in 1813. In 1865-70 it made the mistake of going to war with Argentina, Uruguay and Brazil. Over half the population was killed - leaving 200,000 women and just 28,000 men in the country.

Chaco country

The province of Chaco is a huge area of grassland, swamp and forest. The Gran Chaco to the north is a wilderness about the size of Britain. It is a national park.

Axe breaker

A famous tree of the Gran Chaco tree is called the quebraco ('axe breaker') because the wood is so hard. The wood is rich in tannin, which is used to cure leather.

Dam big

The huge Itaipu hydroelectric dam, on the Paràna River produces more electricity than any other dam in the world. It was completed in 1982. The Guairá Falls - one of the world's largest waterfalls, with twice the volume of water of the Niagara Falls - were completely submerged in the lake created by the dam.

The barrios

Like many cities in South America, the outskirts of the capital of Paraguay, Asunción, include crowded shanty towns called barrios, where the poor live. Most of the houses are shacks, and have no electricity or running water.

BOLIVIA

City of peace
The capital of Bolivia is 3627 m above sea level -
the highest capital in the world. Its full name is
La Paz de Ayacucho ('The Peace of Ayacucho').

The Liberator
Bolivia is named after Simón Bolívar (1783-1830).
From 1811 he led a war against the Spanish rulers,
and helped to push them out of Venezuela,
Colombia, Peru and Ecuador. By 1825 Spanish
rule in South America had come to an end.
Bolívar's dream was to unite South America as
a single country.

Women in bowler hats
About half of the Bolivian population are Indians.
Many live in the capital, but others live in villages
of thatched mud brick
houses, growing maize
and potatoes. The
women wear brightly
coloured woven shawls
and hats which resemble
bowler hats.

The reed boats of Titicaca

Lake Titicaca is the largest lake in South America, covering 8786 sq km. At 3812 m above sea level, it is also the highest lake in the world on which ships operate. The Indians who live beside Lake Titicaca still use traditional boats made with bundles of reeds.

The end of a revolutionary

Ernesto 'Che' Guevara (1928-67) was a Communist revolutionary leader who became a folk hero. Born in Argentina, he helped Fidel Castro to overthrow the government in Cuba in 1959. In 1965 he tried to start a revolution in Bolivia - the poorest country in South America - but was killed by the Bolivian army.

BRAZIL

Portuguese and big
Brazil is by far the largest country in South America. Here the language is Portuguese.

Carnival
Rio de Janeiro is famous for the lavish carnival that it holds each year before the beginning of Lent.

For five days and nights the city throbs to the sound of samba music as thousands of people take part in spectacular parades and street parties.

Under the arms of Christ
A huge statue of Christ stands on top of one of the domed peaks that overlook Rio de Janeiro, 710 m above the level of the sea. Another famous landmark is called the Sugar Loaf Mountain, which rises up from the sea like the tip of a huge finger.

City in the shape of an aeroplane

Rio de Janeiro was the capital of Brazil until 1960.
Then the capital was moved to the brand new city
of Brasília, nearer to the centre of the country.
The groundplan of the city is in the shape of an
aeroplane, with the presidential palace at the tip
of the nose.

The biggest city

With its population of 30 million, São Paulo is
the biggest city in South America. It is a major
industrial centre, producing cars, electrical goods
and textiles, and processing coffee, cocoa, cotton,
and sugar.

Brazil nuts and names

As you might guess, Brazil
nuts come from Brazil.
The trees grow to a great
height, and the nuts
are found inside hard
grapefruit-sized pods.
But another tree gave
Brazil its name.
The caesalpinia tree
produces a reddish
wood used in cabinet-
making. This was called
brasil by the Spanish,
after brasa, meaning
glowing coals - a reference
to the colour of the wood.

Slave lands

Between the 16th and the 19th century, the Portuguese brought about 4 million African slaves to Brazil, mainly to work on the sugar and cocoa plantations. Slavery was abolished in Brazil only in 1888.

The melting pot

The population of Brazil is composed of countless different peoples: the native Indians, Portuguese, Germans, Africans, Asians, Arabs, Chinese, Japanese... and more.

A car that runs on sugar

Brazil has a troubled economy - with far too many imports and not enough exports. As a way of reducing the consumption of petrol, a car was developed that could run on alcohol distilled from sugar cane. Unfortunately, the experiment has not been a success.

Swarming gold mine

Gold has been found in Serra Pelada - and now the region has been turned into a muddy anthill by some 30,000 prospectors called garampeiros. Over 30 million kilograms of gold has so far been found there.

King of coffee, king of iron
Brazil is the world's largest producer of coffee - over 4 million tons a year. It also has the world's largest reserves of iron ore.

Unbeaten football record
Brazil is the only country to have taken part in every finals tournament of the World Cup since the competition started in 1930. It has won the competition three times, in 1958, 1962 and 1970. Brazil's most celebrated player, Pelé, was in the Brazilian team on all three occasions.

Top drivers
Brazil has produced three Formula 1 motor-racing champions: Emerson Fittipaldi (world champion 1972, 1974), Nelson Piquet (1981, 1983, 1987), and Ayrton Senna (1988, 1990, 1991).

The mighty Amazon
The Amazon has 15,000 tributaries, seven of which are major rivers in themselves and over 1600 km long. The Amazon basin drains an area the size of Australia.

Coffee and cream
For most of its length the Amazon is the colour of milky coffee. However, one of its tributaries, called the Rio Negro (Black River) is a translucent black colour. Where the two rivers meet near Manaus, the colours swirl together in what is called the 'Wedding of the Waters'.

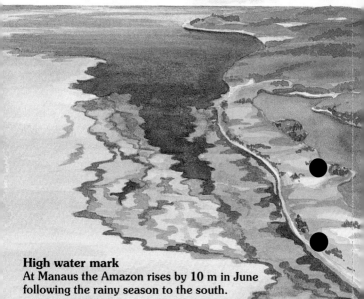

High water mark
At Manaus the Amazon rises by 10 m in June following the rainy season to the south.

Country-sized island
Marajo, an island in the Amazon delta, is as big as Switzerland.

Rubber barons

The rubber tree used to grow mainly in the Amazon basin. From 1839, rubber was widely used for the tyres of carriages and bicycles. The Brazilians who controlled the rubber trade in the Amazon region became immensely rich, and their capital Manaus developed as a wealthy river port. In 1896 a magnificent opera house, the Teatro Amazonas, was built in Manaus, surrounded by the Amazon jungle and great European opera singers, such as Enric Caruso, came to perform here.

The theft of rubber

The Brazilians were careful to protect their valuable trade in rubber, but in 1876 a British botanist called Sir Henry Wickham smuggled out some seeds. These were planted in Kew Gardens, London, and in the 1890s rubber plants were taken to Malaya. From these, the huge British rubber plantations developed, ruining the much more modest Brazilian rubber industry.

Hot and sticky

The temperature in the Amazon Basin doesn't change much throughout the year. It rains for about 200 days every year, and the annual average rainfall is over 200 cm.

The world's greatest rainforest
The Amazon Basin contains half of the world's tropical forest. Giant kapok or silk-cotton trees and para nut trees stretch up to over 60 m, their upper branches covered with bromeliads, lianas, ferns and orchids.

A living Noah's Ark
Here are just a few of the thousands of animal species in the Amazon basin: jaguars, giant otters, howler monkeys, woolly monkeys, anteaters, porcupines, sloths, tapirs, armadillos, capybaras, iguanas, 'poison arrow' frogs, crocodiles and caymans, harpy eagles, macaws, toucans, humming birds, tarantulas, army ants.

Killer fish
The Amazon contains over 2500 species of fish, providing a rich food source. But fishermen have to take care: the Amazon contains freshwater sharks up to 3 m long, stingrays, and electric eels which can deliver an electric shock of 500 volts. But the most famous dangerous fish is the small, but flesh-loving piranha. A shoal of piranhas will strip a carcass to the bones in seconds.

Ancient and modern

Various peoples - such as the Kayapo and Yanomani - still live traditional lives in the Amazon basin. They hunt and fish, and live in villages of thatched houses. However, most have had contact with the outside world - so T-shirts, outboard motors and plastic washing-up bowls may also play a part in their lives.

Disappearing world

The Amazon rainforest is under threat from logging, and from forest clearances to create farm land for crops and cattle ranches.

An estimated 8 million hectares of forest are lost each year. Sadly, the ground cleared for farming does not remain fertile for long - so within a few years farmers have to clear more land, leaving a wasteland behind them.

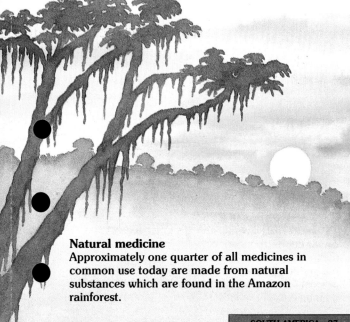

Natural medicine

Approximately one quarter of all medicines in common use today are made from natural substances which are found in the Amazon rainforest.

PERU

Inca capital

The Incas created one of the great early
civilisations of the Americas. Their empire was
based at Cuzco in Peru, but stretched north to
Ecuador and south to Chile. They built palaces,
temples and fortifications out of vast stones, cut to
irregular shapes with stone hammers, but fitted
together with pin-point precision.

Murder and trickery

The Spanish conquistador Hernén Cortés (1476-
1541) managed to conquer the Incas with just 185
men. In 1533 he lured the Inca king Atahualpa to
a meeting, then took him prisoner when he refused
to declare himself Christian. As a ransom, the Incas
had to fill a room with gold and silver, which they
did. But Cortés killed Atahualpa anyway,
and the Inca empire then collapsed.

Gold and pottery

The Incas made ornaments, jewellry, even fish-
hooks and needles out of gold. Much of this was
melted down by the Spanish in the 16th century,
but some splendid pieces have survived. Their
pottery figures also demonstrate the fertile
imagination of the Inca craftsmen.

River trip to Peru
The Amazon is deep enough for ocean-going ships to travel 3200 km, right across Brazil, to the port of Iquitos in Peru, to the east of the Andes. The source of the Amazon is in a series of lakes fed by glaciers high in the Andes of Peru - and just 190 km from the Pacific Ocean.

From rubber to oil
In the 19th century Iquitos became rich from rubber. Its extravagant town hall was designed by Gustav Eiffel (1832-1923) who built the Eiffel tower - and all the building materials were brought up the Amazon from France. The rubber market collapsed at the end of the 19th century, but a new commodity has come to replace it in this region: oil.

Flight of the condor
The condor is the great bird of the Andes, with a vast wingspan of up to 3.2 m wide. Condors are a kind a vulture: they eat carrion - the carcasses of dead animals.

Indian corn

There are over 50 Indian tribes in Peru, and the Indian languages of Quechua and Aimara are spoken by some 2 million people. Most of them work on the land, growing the old Inca crop, maize (or sweet corn).

The music of the Andes

One of the most haunting sounds of the Andes is the music of the panpipes - a set of bamboo tubes, each with a different note, blown from above to produce a clear, resonant sound.

Landscape drawing

Strange patterns and animal shapes have been drawn into the surface of the desert around Nazca - some over 2 km across. No one knows who drew these lines, or why. They are probably about 5000 years old, and may relate to astronomical observations.

Cousin of the camel

The most famous animal of the Andes is the llama. It belongs to the same family as the camel. Llamas are used as pack-animals. Alpacas and vicuñas are similar animals, reared for the high quality of their wool.

Guinea pig for dinner

Guinea pigs come originally from South America. The Incas kept them, not as pets but as a source of food.

Anchovies

Peru has a large fishing fleet, which works among the shoals of fish brought in on the cold Peruvian Current. Anchovies and sardines make up most of the catch.

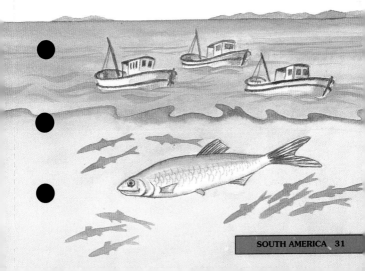

ECUADOR

Equator
Ecuador means Equator. The Equator runs through the north of the country.

City of churches
Quito, the capital of Ecuador, is an old Inca town, which was taken over by the Spanish in 1534. It contains dozens of splendid churches in the Spanish colonial style.

The interiors are richly decorated with gilded columns, shrines, ornate ironwork and statues of the saints.

Volcanoes
Ecuador is regularly shaken by the shudder of an erupting volcano. It has over 30 active volcanoes, including the highest in the world: Cotopaxi (5896 m). The last time it erupted was in 1877.

Jungle oil

Oil is extracted in the hot and forested region of eastern Ecuador, beneath the Andes.

Going bananas

Ecuador is the world's largest producer of dried bananas. Most of the bananas are grown in the hot coastal region, and shipped out through Guayaquil - Ecuador's largest city.

Indian markets

The town of Otavalo, close to the Equator, is famous for its Indian market. Indians come down from the villages in the surrounding hills to sell food, sheep and pigs, and woven rugs and tapestries.

The men wear trilby hats and short white trousers, and the women wear turban-like headdresses of blue cloth and piles of silver-coloured jewellry around their necks.

Unique wildlife

The Galápagos Islands lie 310 km west. There are 12 large islands and hundreds of small ones. They are inhabited by about 6000 people - as well as the unique range of wildlife which has made them famous.

Origin of the species

British scientist Charles Darwin made some of his most important discoveries on the Galápagos Islands. In 1835, he noticed how some of the animals, such as tortoises and finches, had adapted to the island environment. These observations helped to confirm his theory of natural selection. He published these ideas in his book On the Origin of Species by Natural Selection in 1859.

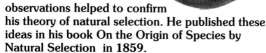

Tortoise islands

Galápago means tortoise in Spanish, and the Galápagos Islands are named after the giant tortoises there. Like a large number of animal species on the islands, these tortoises are found nowhere else on Earth.

Swimming lizards
The large marine iguanas of the Galápagos Islands are the only lizards in the world that swim in the sea in search of their food - seaweed.

Grounded seabirds
Cormorants in most parts of the world are agile seabirds which scud across the surface of the water and swim in the sea to fish. The cormorants of the Galápagos Islands, however, have lost the ability to fly - their wings are too small.

Huge worms
The Galápagos Islands are volcanic, and hot springs still well up under the sea.
In 1977 an American deep-sea research vessel discovered huge worms beside these volcanic vents - 3.5 m long and 3.5 cm thick. They were 3 km below the surface and living in darkness. Such creatures had never been seen before.

COLOMBIA

Colombian gold

Various Indian peoples - such as the Muisca (or Chibcha) and Quimbaya - lived in the Colombian region before and during the Inca period. They made countless objects out of gold, such as earrings, necklaces, ornaments and figurines. Some 25,000 of these have survived, and are kept in the Gold Museum of Colombia's capital Bogotá.

The gold of El Dorado

The Spanish conquistadors were greedy for gold, which they found in great quantities in South America. They had heard the story of El Dorado - the 'Golden Man' - who they believed ruled a kingdom of gold. Despite their long and exhausting searches, they never found El Dorado. Perhaps they had misunderstood stories about a ritual at Lake Guatavita, near Bogotá. Here, each year, the local Indian ruler used to be coated in gold dust and set on a raft to make an offering to the gods.

Gold port
The historic port of Cartagena, also on the Caribbean coast, was built in 1533 as the main port for the Spanish during their conquest of South America. Canons still line the mighty ramparts, overlooking the harbour where galleons, filled with gold and silver, left for Spain.

Crazy city
Colombia has two coasts, one on the Caribbean Sea, and the other on the Pacific. Barranquilla is its largest port, on the Caribbean side. Each year, before Lent, it holds an exuberant carnival, which has earned it the name la ciudad loca ('the crazy city').

Rich and dark
Colombia grows some of the finest coffee in the world, and this is its main export. The fleshy parts of the coffee berry are removed by washing and fermenting; then the beans are dried in the sun. The beans are usually roasted before they are ground up to make coffee.

Orchid capital
Medéllin, the second largest city in Colombia, cultivates orchids and claims to be the 'orchid capital of the world'.

Pop-up books
Many of Europe's most popular lift-the-flap and pop-up books for children have been printed and assembled in Colombia.

Bull-fighting
Most South American countries have maintained the old Spanish tradition of bull-fighting. There is a famous bull-ring in the town of Manizales in E. Colombia - a centre for the coffee-growing industry.

Standard fare
In the cheaper restaurants of Colombia customers receive the standard dish of the day, called simply la comida (the meal). It usually consists of a piece of grilled meat, some rice and salad, and some fried plantain (a banana-like fruit).

Black gold
Colombia is the largest producer of coal in South America. The main deposits are near the town of Riohacha, on the Caribbean coast. Oil has also been found close to the Venezuelan border.

Pan-American highway
This road runs almost the entire length of the Americas, from Alaska to Santiago in Chile and Buenos Aires in Argentina. It passes through some spectacular Andean scenery in Colombia. This is not always a grand motorway, but often a dusty, snaking road. The Highway is used by lorries and by the thousands of buses that travel long distances across South America.

Ancient Indian statues
In the countryside and wooded valleys around the small S. Colombian town of San Agustín stand numerous stone statues, often guarding the sites of tombs. Many of them are well over 1000 years old.

VENEZUELA

Richest in South America
The discovery of oil in 1922 has brought great
wealth to Venezuela - although it is not evenly
shared among its people. Most of the oil comes
from the west, in and around Lake Maracaibo,
a shallow inlet of the Caribbean Sea, where there
are over 10,000 derricks.

Shrine to Bolívar
Simón Bolívar, 'the Liberator' of South America,
was born in Caracas in 1783, and was buried there
in the Panteón Nacional after his death in 1830.

Little Venice
That is what Venezuela means. It was given this
name by the Italian navigator Amerigo Vespucci.
In 1499 he saw the houses of the Paraujano
Indians, built over water on stilts, which reminded
him of the Italian city of Venice.

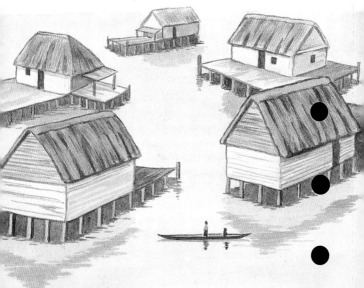

Falling Angel

The highest waterfall in the world is the Salto Angel in southern Venezuela. Water drops in a thin trail down a rockface from a height of 979 m. The falls are named after the American pilot who discovered them in 1933, Jimmy Angel.

The Lost World

Salto Angel is in the Guiana Highlands, a remote and barely accessible region of towering flat-topped mountains called *tepuis*. All kinds of plant-life grows on these flat tops, watered by the abundant rains. This landscape inspired Sir Arthur Conan Doyle to write his novel The Lost World (1912), in which prehistoric plants and dinosaurs are discovered, having survived in isolation for millions of years.

Longest journey on a rope

The Teleférico Mérida is the world's longest passenger-carrying cable car. It travels between the city of Mérida to the top of Pico Espejo (4773 m) - over a distance of 12.8 km.

Peninsular Indians

The Guajira Indians live on the peninsula to the west of Lake Maracaibo, territory shared between Venezuela and Colombia. They live by herding goats and cattle, and fishing. The women dress in distinctive black robes.

Red flash

A beautiful bright red, stork-like bird called the scarlet ibis is found around the coasts of Venezuela - often in large flocks.

Pearl of the Caribbean

Isla Margarita is a gentle, beautiful island of fishing villages and beautiful white sand beaches. It has now also become a popular holiday resort.
Oyster pearls are found in the waters around the island - hence its name: margarita means pearl in Spanish.

Cattle country

The dismal llanos plains of central Venezuela provide vast grazing grounds for herds of hump-backed zebu cattle. These cattle originated in India, so can withstand the hot, dry climate. They are looked after by cowboys called llaneros.

National dance

The joropa is the national dance of Venezuela, performed by llaneros and their partners. The men wear white linen suits, and the women wear broad skirts. The dance is accompanied by music played on a harp, a small four-stringed guitar called a *cuadra*, and maracas - dried gourds filled with seeds.

National dish

The most famous dish of Venezuela is pabellón - flaked beef served with black beans, wild rice, fried plantains and *arepas* (cornflour rolls).

GUYANA

Odd one out
Guyana is the only English-speaking country in
South America. Guyana gained its independence
from Britain in 1966.

Sugar river
The name Guyana means 'land of many waters'.
One of these rivers became so famous for the
brown sugar that was produced on its banks that
this kind of sugar was named after it: Demerara.

Six into one
Several different
peoples live in Guyana.
The Carib Indians are
the original inhabitants.
The Dutch, French and
British brought in
African slaves. After
the abolition of
slavery Portuguese
and Chinese labourers
were encouraged
to settle here. And
Asians from India
followed in large
numbers, and now
make up the largest
community in
the country.

Wooden city
Georgetown is largely made of wooden buildings - many of them, such as the cathedral, fine examples of this historic style of Caribbean architecture.

Rice pudding
The main crop of Guyana is sugar cane. The second most important crop is rice.

Spectacular falls
The Kaieteur Falls on the River Potaro are 90 m wide and fall 226 m in a single sheet of water - over four times the height of the Niagara Falls.

Where bauxite is king
The most important export of Guyana is bauxite - aluminium ore. Guyana also produces gold, diamonds, manganese and uranium.

SURINAME

Dutch South America
Surinam was a Dutch colony called Dutch Guiana until 1975, when it declared independence and became the South America's newest independent state. The Dutch influence can still be seen in the style of some of the buildings in the capital, Paramaribo.

Hindu temples
A quarter of the population of Surinam is Hindu - mainly people of Indian origin who arrived in the 19th century. Paramaribo has a number of Hindu temples.

Mass exodus
Surinam is a poor country, and many people have left it to seek work elsewhere. About half the entire population left the country in the 1970s, most of them going to the Netherlands.

Same mix, but different
Like Guyana, the main crops are sugar and rice. Oranges, coffee, coconuts, cocoa and bananas are also grown. Like Guyana, also, bauxite is the major export.

East of Java
The Dutch built a new settlement on the coast of Dutch Guiana which they called New Amsterdam. At this time they also ruled Indonesia. A large community of Indonesians from Java settled in New Amsterdam, and is living there still.

Eggs in the sand
There are only two known places in the world where giant leatherback turtles come to lay their eggs: one is in Malaysia and the other is in Surinam. The female turtles clamber up the beach by night, and lay their eggs in the sand. Leatherback turtles are the largest turtles in the world, measuring over 2 m in length and weighing up to 450 kg.

FRENCH GUIANA

France in South America
French Guiana - or Guyane, as it is known in
French - is the last remaining European overseas
territory in South America.
It is in fact a department of France, and sends
representatives to the National Assembly in Paris.

Cayenne pepper
The capital of French Guiana is the main port,
Cayenne. The kind of hot chilli powder called
cayenne pepper is named after the town.

Devil's Island
This island off the coast of French Guiana was used
by the French as a prison colony for hardened
criminals from 1852 to 1939. Conditions were very
harsh - and it was virtually impossible to escape.